About This Book

Title: *Dog or Cat?*

Step: 1

Word Count: 91

Skills in Focus: All short vowels

Tricky Words: nose, tail, from, you, fur, are

Ideas For Using This Book

Before Reading:

- **Comprehension:** Look at the title and cover image together. Ask readers what they know about dogs and cats. What new things do they think they might learn in this book?
- **Accuracy:** Practice saying the tricky words listed on page 1.
- **Phonics and Phonemic Awareness:** Have readers point to the word *dog* in the title. Practice taking apart and putting together the sounds. Ask readers to tap a new finger to their thumb to count the sounds they hear. Ask: How many sounds are in the word *dog*? What is the first sound? Middle sound? End sound? Change the /d/ to /l/. What word is it? Repeat with the word *cat*. Change the /c/ to /m/. What other *-at* words do readers know?

During Reading:

- Have readers point under each word as they read it.
- **Decoding:** If readers are stuck on a word, help them say each sound and blend the sounds together smoothly. Be sure to point out any short vowel sounds.
- **Comprehension:** Invite students to talk about what new things they are learning about dogs and cats while reading. What are they learning that they didn't know before?

After Reading:

Discuss the book. Some ideas for questions:

- Do you have a cat or dog as a pet? Do you know someone who has a pet dog or cat?
- Do you like dogs or cats better? Why?

Dog or Cat?

Text by Laura Stickney

Reading Consultant
Deborah MacPhee, PhD
Professor, School of Teaching and Learning
Illinois State University

PICTURE WINDOW BOOKS
a capstone imprint

Dogs and cats are pets.

Dogs can get big.

A dog has fur.
Its nose is wet.

A dog can wag its tail. It can run.

Dogs can sit.
Dogs can beg.

Dogs can hop up.

Cats are not as big as dogs.

Cats can be red.
Cats can be tan.

Cats can rub on kids' legs.

A cat licks its fur.
Cats lap from cups.

Cats nap in beds.

Cats hop. Cats sit on rugs.

Will you get a dog or cat?

More Ideas:

Phonemic Awareness Activity

Practicing Short Vowels:
Say a short vowel story word for readers to practice segmenting the sounds. Tell the readers to hop in place as they break apart the word, with one hop for each sound they say. Begin with *dog*. They will hop once for /d/, again for /o/, and once more for /g/. Ask: What was the first sound? Middle sound? Ending sound? Optional: Readers can clap or tap for each sound instead.

Suggested words:
- lick
- nap
- cup
- pet
- cat

Extended Learning Activity

Play Pretend:
Ask readers to imagine that they have a pet dog or cat. Have them draw a picture of the pet on a piece of paper. Then ask readers to write three sentences about the pet. Have students use words with short vowel sounds in their sentences.

Published by Picture Window Books, an imprint of Capstone
1710 Roe Crest Drive, North Mankato, Minnesota 56003
capstonepub.com

Copyright © 2026 by Capstone.
All rights reserved. No part of this publication may be reproduced in whole or in part, or stored in a retrieval system, or transmitted in any form or by any means, electronic, mechanical, photocopying, recording, or otherwise, without written permission of the publisher.

Library of Congress Cataloging-in-Publication Data is available on the Library of Congress website.

ISBN: 9798875226946 (hardback)
ISBN: 9798875229138 (paperback)
ISBN: 9798875229114 (eBook PDF)

Image Credits: iStock: Domepitipat, 1, 19, FatCamera, 2–3, IG_Royal, 18, Infinityyy, 6–7, LightFieldStudios, 4–5; Shutterstock: Anna Averianova, cover, arturs.stiebrins, 9, Eric Isselee, 8, Erika Mizikaite, 21, Image bug, 11, Jaromir Chalabala, 14–15, 24, Laksena, 16–17, Oksana Shufrych, 22–23, Pixel-Shot, 12–13, Rawpixel.com, 10, tickcharoen04, 20

Printed and bound in China. 6274